In Conversation

Vaisakh Mohandas

BookLeaf Publishing

India | USA | UK

Made with ❤ on the BookLeaf Publishing Platform
www.bookleafpub.in
www.bookleafpub.com

Dedication

For Love

Preface

I never wanted to be a poet. Yet here I am, claiming to be one as I fill in pages after pages of words spoken straight from the soul. It might be flawed, it might not be- it's all your perception. At the end of the day, subjectivity rules- and that is something we tend to ignore.

Here are a collection of poems, many heart-rending, still many others playing with some semblance of beauty. It amazes me still how wonderfully I can portray sadness- in my eyes, of course; you may think different- for there is nothing that has ruled me ever so more than sadness. My friends call me the "intellectual sad man" for a reason, eh?

Anyhow, enjoy. Do let me know what you think about this. I will accept every word with an open heart. Bon voyage!

Acknowledgements

I dedicate this book to everyone who's been with me through thick-and-thin- my parents, my family, my friends, my teachers, my past lovers. All have given me a piece to this puzzle of writing that I still continue to join. This is but a mere step in achieving the full picture. Will I ever? No one really knows, right? Time will tell. It always does.

Thanks to BookLeafPublishing for giving me this honor. It was quite a fun, writing one poem everyday. A challenge, of course, but the best challenges are the ones that are fun- and make you learn something along the way. I seem to have found both within this.

Finally, thanks to every book and every written word that I have processed, for without you I would be nothing. Nothing at all. I'm glad I'm something. Who wouldn't be?

I. Angelo Della Morte
(Angel of Death)

I speak no Italian
But the words embody
The spirits that run
Astray in our world today

Angel of Death
Angels of Death?
Fly like vultures
Feasts on prey

Because so much hate
Floods from every crevice
Of this (un)holy Earth
Seeping through minds, delusions rife

We sleep when others cry
We laugh while others die
We do nothing, but speak of something
To do something while we can indeed do nothing

Watch, heavens, as the world so proclaimed to be
The cradle of civilization
Smother its own seeds
Sown by them, themselves

I speak like I know something
But all I can do is speak like I know something
I can never imagine to know
The workings of this (un)holy world

But, I am grown enough, friends
To realize that dark times are coming
For some, dark times are here
For some, there is only pain

Why do I speak
Like I can fathom
The darkness that cradles
The cradle of civilization?

This is but a ramble
Of a mind grown madder
This is of no importance
I speak madness

It might make sense to you, reader

I am but words on paper
Singing you a (non)sensical hymn
I am but words on paper

Angelo della morte (Angel of Death)
Vieni da me ora (Come to me now)
Prendimi dalla mia miseria (Take me out of my misery)
Paradiso o inferno, vado. (Paradise or hell, I go.)

II. Who Would I Be, If I Am Not With She?

How wonderful it is that I don't have to speak a word
For you to understand what exactly I mean
How do you do this? How do you glean from me my feelings so clean?
Whenever I ask you so, you smile; you know exactly, sweet bird
You have this ability to heal me, to make me heard
I don't understand how I am seen
All I know is that I am seen
And, Gods, am I grateful for you, beautiful bird

I love you, that I vow
You love me, that I see
And so when anyone asks me who I am to be
I reply, "Now, now..."
"Who would I be, if I am not with she? How would I live? Who would I hold?"
Perhaps it has been foretold, for to you I have my soul sold.

III. Rip Me

Rip me a new skin, will you?
I'm tired of hating myself
I'm tired of looking at the mirror every night
Wishing to be someone else

Rip out my eyeballs, will you?
What I see everyday
I'm tired of seeing it
Endless fury and hate

Rip me from my life, will you?
I'm surrounded by two-faced crooks
Who want nothing more from me than my money
I'm broke, b*****s!

Rip me a new heart, will you?
I'm tired of feeling with this one
I want to wear my heart on my sleeve
I don't want it in a casket, locked and hidden forever

Where's the key?
The key to your heart
I lost it forever, I said
In some alley, in some town

I whimper every night
I don't want to do this, I don't
So rip me apart, won't you?
I'm tired of it all.

IV. Diminish Me If You Will (Villanelle)

Diminish me if you will, Father
Drench me in your sorrows unfairly
You're in pain, I gather

Scare me, you can try, or don't bother
I bow before your might, rarely
Diminish me if you will, Father

I know you'd rather
Steer me like your boats, that scrape by barely
You're in pain, I gather

Yet I must say, today, this heather
That waves so freely, waves freer as I escape you sparely
Diminish me if you will, Father

You try your best, you will to tether
Me here in this village, I hate so much, so squarely
You're in pain, I gather

No matter though, what you do, Father
You will be in my memories, never rarely
Diminish me if you will, Father
You're in pain, I gather.

V. Vehemence

Have you heard the story
Of Prometheus, the god?

How he gave us fire,
Much to Zeus' ire?

How he was bound to rock
While a vulture ate his insides?

Does that mean to evolve is to sin?
I know not, my dears.

Maybe it explains
The fire that burns within

This passion that licks and smolders
Inside my husk of flesh

This warmth that crackles and pops
Inside my soul's embrace

This is a dangerous fire, my dears
It makes logic ill
It makes me shiver
Aching for a rush of water

Sometimes it eats me up
Much like the vultures to the corpse

Sometimes it chains me down
Much like Prometheus, to that rock

How could this fire be
So vehemently vitriolic?
So virtuously vainglorious?
So violently voluptuous?
So vibrantly vicarious?

Maybe Zeus was correct
Without this fire, we would not pain

Maybe Prometheus was wrong
With this fire, why do we pain?

Answer me, my dears
Why do we pain?

VI. Light

I glimpse a light at the end of the tunnel
It beckons me, a lighthouse to the weary seafarer.

A hand reaches to me from the void
I clasp it and, around me, roses flower.

An embrace like a soft blanket lays heavy around me
The touch is electric- sparks that fuel wildfires emerge.

Not even Hades could pull me back down
The gravity could reverse, the vacuum of space may
consume me

Still I will stay, rooted like the five-hundred year oak
For I have found where I belong.

Fear me, my troubles
There is not a nook to which you can usher me.
There is not a crevice to which you can prison me.
There is not a rock to which you can chain me.

Fear me, my troubles
For now, I do not fear myself.

VII. Crochet

The crochet hook lies untouched
It will rust; it should be put away.

The wicker chair rocks
It creaks and it groans
It is loud; it must be stopped.

The winter breeze slips through the room
The door is open; it should be shut.

The newspaper ruffles and flaps
Where is the paper-weight? It must be put.

The TV plays, drama-rich
It must be turned off; the time is up.

The black cat jumps into the house
It meows; it wants some milk.

It sneaks to its bowl, silver enshrined.

The green eyes; they gaze inside.

It is empty; it must be filled.
But who will fill it?

Outside, there are sounds.
Some loud; some hushed.

A wail pierces the air.
The cat; it looks up.

The orange sun; it begins setting.
The wrinkled feet disappear; the ambulance is here.

VIII. summertime springwater

The words that fall from your tongue
Sound like summertime springwater

The sparks that buzz from your touch
Feel like a gentle autumn breeze

The gaze that pierces from your eyes
Melts me like springtime ice-blocks

The kiss that your lips give to mine
Tastes like wintry hot chocolate

The time that I spend with you
Seasons go by in a flash

The days that I hold you
Are angelic in their divinity

The moments that we lie together

Not even Zeus could pull me from you

This life that I live with you
Is a life in tranquil paradise

This life that I live with you
Will only end when I die with you.

And still it will go on.

IX. come what may

Come what may
The storm might have passed
Or it is yet to arrive

Come what may
Hell might drag you back in
The devil won't let go of your ankles

Come what may
The earth might shatter into a billion shards
The oceans might flood us miles below

Come what may,
I will be by your side.

I will sail the storms that bellow and rage with you.
I will fight the devil with chains and swords with you.
I will hold together the crumbling world for you.

A thousand arrows could pierce my flesh,

A dozen mighty beasts may peck at my heart,
A hundred words could shred my brain,
Still I will be there with you.

You might wish to loathe yourself.
I will tell you,
You must not.
You are perfect.

You are as perfect
As the moon over the beck of the magical river,
Bathing the world in silver as beauty itself.
As the sun closing its eyes,
Releasing hues of a million waves,
Coloring the sky a parade.

Come what may, my friend,
Come what may.
It is not enough to halt us.

X. xylophone

A symphony of tears
Play across my face
This is beauty, I think
This is it.

My worries are quelled
And my fears are squashed
This is a kind of happiness
Compared to blooming flowers.

As the mallet strikes the wooden
And the magic strikes the ears,
You find a peace
Akin to standing amidst fields of cotton,
Emptiness in all directions.

If I could weave such a tapestry,
With wondrous harmonies
Not whimsical wool,
I could conquer the hearts

And the souls of this world.

Alas, I cannot
So I sit and I sigh
As the xylophone
Sings me a melody of heart.

XI. the things i'd do for u

The things I'd do for you
Number amongst infinity
That's how much I'll give for you

I'll give you the universe
Where everything exists
Because my everything is you.

I'll write scriptures and tabloids
Etched in the devotion of you.

I'll carve inscriptions into pillars
Eternal in the benevolence of you.

So sweet is your presence
That is nectar to the divine
Ambrosia to the demigods
And elixir to me.

So soft is your gaze

That is shelter for the homeless
Food for the hungry
And heaven true to me.

The things I'd do for you
Number not just in the infinity
But in the measures of all
That is quantifiable.

The things I'd do for you
I'd do forever.

Ad vitam aeternam (To eternal life)
Et ad amor aeternam. (And to eternal love.)

XII. helena

Helena, with your ferocity,
You could turn any man
Into a groveling miser
Who begs at your rubber
For a peace only you can give.

Helena, with your luminescence
And the velvet colored plates
That cover you like armor,
Any man would thirst
For a feel of your power.

Helena, with your voice,
The gentle rumble and the glorious roar
Any man would be filled
With warmness like melted chocolate
Heaven must sound like this.

As I lay my hands on this rubber that breathes,
As I feel the soul fueling beneath my feet,

As my foot presses against the metal plate,
As the wind beats a rhythm into my face,
I find you, Helena, a dream come true.

As the gears turn and the axle rotates,
As the exhausts boom and crackle, fire,
As the engine sings and hums, melody,
As the adrenaline rushes, fury,
I find you, Helena, beauty tenfold.

XIII. fairytale

When she smiles, it's heaven come down
When she laughs, it's Orpheus reincarnate

Her eyes, they stare so intently
A man could not help but weaken

Her fingers, they touch me so gentle
A melody played on my arms

She's a dream that is born out of dreams
A fantasy in reality, an angel in hell

When she walks, the earth mother sings
When she talks, the skies, they sing

Her embrace, eternally ethereal
Leaves me pining, pitifully pale

Her hair, it curls and it swivels
A cloud, soft as cotton

She would be mine if she wanted
I would be hers if she wanted

But for now, she's nothing but
A glimpse of a fairytale heaven.

XIV. amber

Her eyes were a liquid amber
His were a stone-cold blue

Her hands played a melody of whispers
His played a percussive roar

Her tongue spoke a gentle cabaret
His spoke a language vaudevillian

Her heart beat a steady rhythm
His beat a frantic chaos

She dreams of a man, gentle as she
He of a woman, gentle as she

Both tread a path with opposite bearings
Will they meet or will they not?

XV. ETERNALITY

Eternal longing bears no fruit
I've reached up to the branches
And grasped at empty air

Eternal love bears no fruit
My misplaced heart,
Oh where art thou

Eternal suffering, now that,
That is true
To be eternal is to suffer
That is true

You wouldn't understand
The heart that longs for love
Longs for pain, too

You wouldn't know
I step onto thorns
The stems of roses

Aye, what a pain it is
To love something greater
Than yourself

Aye, what a pain it is
To long for something
Like you long for peace

It bears no fruit
Eternality.
It bears no fruit.

XVI. FUTILITY

Withering branches whisper,
Wallowing, they wait,
For a green to grow.

Dry dunes of dust demand
A drop of water to drain
Their sorrows in safety.

Flora and fauna, fall feeling
For futile fantasy is a phantasm,
They die, devoid, alone.

The apex predator
Preys on the avenues
For spare change,
Change no one can spare.

The crying child
Croons like a cockatiel
For the liquid of life

Yet listlessly lie.

What have we become?
Will we become wishful
For water; whole wheat?

While the world wilts,
Will we watch and whine
Or will we wrought a war
To save sentience, soil and sweet?

Maybe it is futile
For a fellow to hope.

Maybe in this futility,
He will be fraught
To fix forever
The forever future.

XVII. BREVITY

How deplorable it is that time passes
Nothing is ever enough
You might wish to conquer
The seven seas
Or to wander the seven realms

Yet there they lie,
Dreams unfulfilled
There they lie,
Listlessly staring into the abyss
One which you created for yourself

When you say nothing matters
Truer words have not been spoken
Nothing matters,
We are but a speck, insignificant
In the universe of a billion years, what are we of one-
hundred?

No, but what is the point of it all?

If death is the answer to life
Then what is the question?
If we all are to die,
Why bother living at all?

Love?
It comes and goes
Transient as it is,
Impermanence is what it is
No one loves forever

Hope?
Hope for what?
For a better tomorrow?
While every minute we spend alive
Is one minute off our life?

Happiness?
What defines happiness?
Money? Love? Success?
Aren't these all transient?
Aren't these all riddled with brevity?

How deplorable is it that we live
When pain is all we get for our fruit
When we know it will all end under the earth

How deplorable is it that we live
Knowing we will cease to exist?

XVIII. SOLILOQUY

At the end of the day, it's always just me.
Sorrow and fear, they collide
And I destroy

At the end of the day, it's always just me.
Crying on the floor of the kitchen
It's always just me

Physicalities tend to be absent
The only physicality is I
Yes, it's always just me

Curling up into a ball, I cry
Arms to reach around me, they-
Coldness embraces me

It's always just me
I'm a shoulder to cry on
Can't cry on your own shoulder now, can you?

At the end of the day, it's always just me.
My eyes search
They fall on nothing

They fall on nothing
But the reflections of the pools of my tears
I look, and it's always just me

At the end of the world,
Will it always just be me?

In the end of my journey,
Will it always just be me?

At the end of the day,
Will it *always* just be me?

XIX. IDOLATRY

You'll find a dark shadow of a hand
Wrapping itself around your beating heart
You'll find it clenching and squeezing
As out oozes the soul with which you live

You'll hear disembodied voices
Whispering in the darkness of the alleys of your mind
Guiding you to drown viciously
In the syrup of a misleading sweet

You'll find you're out of breath
Your gut clenches and collapses in
With every utterance, a hole is made
And mere sand fills it, only to collapse

Even still, why do we love?

If love is so powerful,
Why does it not heal the very wounds it creates?
If love is so ethereal,

Why does it seem so transient?

Idolatry, it is defined as the
Extreme admiration or reverence for something
Why do we idolize pain? Sorrow? Heartbreak?
Maybe because we idolize love.

They are intrinsic, these two.
One cannot exist without the other.

XX . TELEPATHY

Storms try hard to weather me down
Waves ten feet high play a comedy on me
As I'm thrown, one end of the void to the other
Drown, drown in your own misery, they say

Stone-heavy sorrow, tied to me like paperweight
Drag me down into the depths of an abyss
Not even a particle of light could exist down here
Smother, smother in your painful silence, they say

Sharp, serrated edges tattoo onto me agony of loss
As memories I held dear slither away
Not even Apollo could heal these wounds
Burn, burn in your gilded cage, they say

And then I see you.

Our eyes meet for but a second
Every message writ in love
Pass through mine to yours

If only telepathy existed, they'd be yours

If only I could speak to you
If only those words which lay untouched
Which lay ever blossoming love
Escaped the caverns of my mind

And pierced your gentle soul
And maybe make you see
There are no depths I would not go
There is no hell I would not go

For you.

You turn your head
And I turn mine
You go forward, I go back

Plunged am I once more
Into the very hell I create
Away from the very heaven you remain

Plunged am I once more
Into the laments of my soul
Aching for a hand to grasp.

XXI. TAPESTRY

Words weave souls together
An elaborate pattern interlaced with emotion
And the color, not to forget
Shadows and brush strokes of the vitesse

To hold the needle that is the pen
To weave on the fabric that is the paper
Worthy, I may not be
But I will try- harmless as it is

You might say words do not speak much
But my, my, these very words have shattered being
They have eclipsed creation
They have fixed what is broken

And within me the urge still lies
To try to weave to the best I can
A magic and a spell of a frivolous beauty
Grasp meanings as they are, needles to the haystack

As this journey ends, the chapter closed
Eyes open, forge ahead I will
To be upon the world a staunch epiphany
One remembered, inscribed in the inner

Though promises are seldom kept
Let me digress to you this
That tapestries I will weave of beauty, of creation
Will lie eternal, words a-free.